Again Calls the Owl

ALSO BY MARGARET CRAVEN

I Heard the Owl Call My Name
Walk Gently This Good Earth

Again Calls

the Owl

Margaret Craven

Illustrated by Joan Miller

G. P. PUTNAM'S SONS

New York

Designed by Bernard Schleifer

Library of Congress Cataloging in Publication Data

Craven, Margaret.
    Again calls the owl.

    1. Craven, Margaret—Biography. 2. Novelists,
American—20th century—Biography. I. Title.
PS3553.R277Z463   813'.5'4 [B]   79-22388
ISBN 0-399-12453-5

Printed in the United States of America

Third Impression

Again Calls the Owl

WHEN WILSON, MY TWIN BROTHER, and I were still small, our brother Leslie, almost twelve years our senior, was already going to Stanford. He was home from the first war, and there was no need for him to work his way through college. Times were good and no one dreamed of any possible depression.

I have always been touched that when Leslie was at Stanford he wrote little stories to his small brother and sister. I was "Giggle" and Wilson was "Goggle." I remember on one he wrote, "Someday you will write stories like this and you will sell them."

In the summer we always went to the little town of Glacier in the very northwest corner of the country. We rode the cayuse pack ponies, the mountains huge around us. Father promised us that when we were older he would take us to Koma Kulshan, up to the high ridge and show us some of its wonders, where we could look down upon its many glaciers.

Already things were changing a little. Father had been a pioneer in Montana. He was a lawyer and a man of utter integrity. He had an accident. He was not like himself and dropped his life insurance. Soon he had a stroke and was hospitalized for a very long time. He knew no one.

Mother closed the house, sold the law books and furniture, stored the keepsakes and stayed with father.

Wilson and I suddenly realized that we were going to have responsibilities. We took the money that was left, borrowed more and went to Stanford.

The first thing I did was flunk the compulsory English test and I had to take "bonehead," a course in simple composition, and I remember that on one of my entries the woman professor wrote, "I think you will be able to write fiction if you are willing to work hard." In her next class I smiled and she smiled back. Neither of us mentioned it.

There was no professor of creative writing then. If you majored in English, barring miracles, you taught it. I did not major in English. I burned my bridges behind me, majored in history with a minor in economics or political science, I don't remember which, took several biology courses but an insufficient number in any subject to be forced into teaching anything at all.

A fine old newspaper man had retired to return to Stanford for an advanced degree and to teach in the journalism department. When I took his course in journalism he said to me, "I don't know what it takes to make a fiction writer, girl. Whatever it is, you have it. Get a job on a newspaper and begin writing stories on the side."

There were many young people working their way through Stanford then. They came from near and far, from little towns of which I had never heard. The trains no longer stopped at every whistle-stop. Farmers bought the little station houses and carted them away to house their equipment, their cows and sheep. The little towns, once so active and alive, simply disappeared. Except for the big cities, the country was still uncluttered and in some areas lonely. The young, if they were good students and had ambition, sought a fine college—not so easy to come by then—where they could work for the education they were going to need so badly.

Some of the larger eastern state universities had well-established scholarships. Stanford had some for the boys and almost none for the girls unless they combined scholarship with some worthwhile activity. Stanford made the shy, the broke, the determined and the lonely work for the education they needed. In return, youth gave the best it had.

California was the richest state, with no eerie shadow of a depression to come. It still had its campus queens with their pearls, beautiful fluted blouses and cashmere coats. There were only five hundred girls at Stanford. All the freshmen lived in Roble Hall. The next year the pledges would move to the sororities, not yet abolished. It was unthinkable that a fraternity man would date a girl who had no time for activities, no money for a sorority, who went every summer to summer school, carried extra hours, going through Stanford fast as a jackrabbit.

My brother signed tuition notes and rode a bicycle three times a day to wash dishes in a private school in exchange for his meals. One day he fell off and banged his knee. When he went to the infirmary to have it dressed, the doctor said: "Trying to kill yourself, son? It says here on your card you come from Puget Sound, which means you can row, right? Now, I'll tell you what you are going to do. You are going to San Francisco and shut yourself up in some cheap waterfront hotel where the ship crews stay. Buy a midshipman's manual and memorize it. In a week your knee will be entirely healed. Pick a day when some boat comes in and look for a crewman coming along with his gear over his shoulder. Tell him what you want to do and ask him if he will sell you some old clothes for five dollars. He will grin, but he will do it. He will help you choose the ship, one of the smaller Dollar ships probably. You will have no trouble with the union, not yet anyway. Put on the clothes and take the required boat test. If anybody asks you what college you went to, say barber's college. You will start out an ordinary seaman and come back an able-bodied seaman. Don't be surprised if at every port the men ask you to keep their money for them so they won't spend it when they go ashore, if in some Chinese port a little old Chinese woman with jade pins in her hair comes in the fo'c'sle where the men are dressing and undressing, calling softly 'sew, sew.' She is Mary and they love her. They usually bring her some little gift—a bar of fine soap, a small bottle of perfume. They show her the pictures of their girls, and she mends their socks, washes and irons their clothes, sews on the buttons for a few cents."

"How do you know this, sir?" Wilson asked.

"Because I did it. You will find more real democracy at sea than you will ever find here in this fine university and you will come home with some marvelous memories, and when you get back, son, you will be a man."

My brother did it. And it was true. He

painted much of the way to Japan, polished brass, washed down the decks, bleached and sanded them. He ran the holystone, learning to let it slide with the ship's roll. When the ship approached the first port in Japan and the bos'n had the heaving line ready, he said, "Slim, you think you're man enough to reach the dock with it?" My brother gave it everything he had. The heaving line reached the dock, crossed it, and the monkey fist on the end went through a warehouse window with a splintering crash. After that he was known as "Big Slim."

In the Inland Sea of Japan he stood watch on the bow, ringing the bell every half hour to show he was awake, checking the running lights and calling out, "The lights are shining brightly, sir," and listening for the answering "Aye!" He made three trips in all. He came back an able-bodied seaman and the first mate said to him, "Always glad to have you aboard, Big Slim."

At Christmas holiday you could always spot the students who were working their way through school. They hung around the campus because they couldn't afford to go home. We saw little of each other, usually, but during the holidays we invented a most splendid yearly splurge. Wilson would give money he had made at sea. One year, I sold a skirt I didn't like for ten dollars. Or someone's uncle might have sent him a most unexpected check. Every Christmas we would drive to the city in an ancient rattletrap car. We enjoyed a most modest meal and then went to the theater. If we could manage seventy-five cents each, we sat in the back row of the second balcony. If we could only manage fifty cents, we climbed two long flights of stairs and sat in the back of the third balcony. The theaters are still there, the acoustics as good. We heard Otis Skinner, David Warfield, Maude Adams in *The Little Minister*, Jane Cowl in *Romeo and Juliet*, and *The Shanghai Gesture* and all assorted Barrymores. We heard them, but all we saw was the tops of their heads. It was wonderful!

Where there is youth there is always humor. Whatever happened to that blithe, happy sprite, daughter of a famous biologist, who used to smuggle into Roble Hall a large king snake and about the time everybody was through studying and ready for a shower, turn it loose on the highly polished linoleum of the hall? It did not bite, it was a member of the constrictor family. Once, the snake twined itself tenaciously around the girl's right arm. She yelled happily for assistance. We refused unless she promised to return it to its natural habitat and leave it there. When her arm began to turn blue, we helped untangle it. After that she contented herself with emerging from the swimming pool too late to change for dinner. She put on a dress over her wet suit and took the varnish off the chairs while the rest of us hooked our heels around the chair rungs to escape the puddles.

Most of the campus queens sent their fluted blouses out to be laundered, but this cost twenty-five cents apiece—a really enormous sum. Along with all the "boneheads," they washed their undies in the laundry downstairs and hung them on the lines to dry. Though I never saw the honor code broken at Stanford, we had a thief among us who would remove garments drying on the basement lines. After that the queens and nonqueens alike dried their unmentionables on the radiators in their rooms. If you called on a friend in the evening after study, you had to crawl under a clothesline rigged up to hold slips and nightgowns.

You could have with a roommate, two tiny bedrooms and a small shared study, or a room by yourself. I had a single room in front where I could see all that went on.

Sometimes a girl would flunk out or be called home by illness—her room left empty. This was an invitation too tantalizing to resist. Everybody who had nerve enough would enter the room at midnight, carefully open the windows, stuff the crack at the bottom of the door and prepare for the act that meant instant dismissal if caught. No lights were permitted, of course, except those that burned all night outside the dorm. One intrepid soul provided a package of "Melacrinos," kept in perfumed cotton and obviously of vast antiquity. Nobody had yet discovered that cigarettes were harmful to health. They were unladylike, which was worse. We sat on the floor and lit up, carefully catching the ashes in a glass from our room. We were not caught, but we did grow very, very dizzy.

We were assigned seats for meals, eight girls to a table. Sometimes we would talk about what work we wanted to do. I remember at my table seven of the girls wanted to write. I kept still. The food never varied from week to week or season to

season. The woman in charge of feeding us had it
as a concession. Sunday we had rabbit pretending
to be chicken, and ice cream. Thursday night of
every week throughout the year we had prune
whip—a highlight! Once, however, the woman in
charge of feeding us served something that was
spoiled. All the girls at Roble Hall were sick and
united to demand that the authorities change the
system—and we won.

I didn't know it, but I was already gathering
material for my first stories. Every girl was required to know how to swim. The waters of my
home state are so cold no one has ever been able to
swim across the Strait of Juan de Fuca, though it is
considerably narrower than the English Channel.
Most adults refused to stick in even a toe, consider-
ing this an invitation to rheumatism, permanent
and maybe deadly. An occasional remittance man
would dive in and come up gasping for breath as if
he had been walloped in the face with a chunk of
ice. Father informed me that there are things on
this earth only an Englishman will attempt. I

learned to swim at the YWCA in the tank, which was twenty-five feet long. At Stanford I took intermediate followed by advanced swimming.

Our coach was a Norwegian champion. She seldom went in the water but when she did, she was wonderful to behold. She stood on the side of the tank in a nice warm bathrobe and directed operations with a megaphone.

At the end of advanced swimming we were required to prove our skill. I waited my turn fervently praying I would draw some sweet little girl who would be as scared as I was and give me no trouble. No luck! The coach called out a girl who lived on Catalina and could swim twenty miles and had done so often. She weighed at least fifty pounds more than I did and had a glint in her eye of utter confidence. It was to her the coach spoke first. "When I say start, I want you to dive into the twelve-foot-deep end. You, Miss Craven, will follow. You are to break a front stranglehold, bring her up for air, let her go at once and go down after her and break a back stranglehold. Then you are to propel her to the end of the tank and roll her up on the side."

I could see myself being resuscitated probably from death itself. The behemoth whom I was to save looked very pleased, if not smug. She dived in. She did it beautifully. I went after her. Now there is one stranglehold you don't permit yourself to get into if you have gumption, but I was sure this girl would entrap me in it.

She got a front stranglehold. I brought up a knee and whacked her hard in the stomach. I heard the air go out of her, so I held her nose. We came up.

Down she went. Down I went after her. This was the back stranglehold. I got hold of one of her little fingers and bit it, good and hard. I stuck my thumb in her eye.

Above me there seemed to be considerable commotion. The coach was yelling loudly through her megaphone. We came up. I did not waste time lugging this specimen gently to the end of the pool. I snatched off her cap, grabbed her by the hair, and, when we reached the end of the pool, I encouraged her to assist me in rolling her up the side of the tank by pinching her buttocks.

All around the pool the girls were watching and they seemed to look pleased.

"Miss Craven," yelled the coach through her megaphone, "didn't you hear me? You were too rough. Outrageous!"

"I didn't hear a thing," I said when I could get

my breath. "I'm just happy to be alive. After all, that's something."

Years later I used this incident in a story and I sent the coach a copy. On it I wrote, "I owe this one to you."

I was graduated at the end of summer school and made arrangements to have my diploma mailed to me. I applied with considerable confidence at the morning paper, the San Jose *Mercury Herald*, whose managing editor had need of a secretary. He wrote a front page column called "The Editor's Analysis," and each year the students of the local college wrote a takeoff of it called "The Editor's Paralysis."

When I went in, he looked me over carefully from a pair of keen, humorous eyes. He was a Scot, well past sixty, which I considered definitely antique.

"Do you type?" he asked dryly.

"Yes."

"Do you take dictation?"

"Stanford provided a course in dictation to

help students find jobs, without credit, of course."

"Naturally. Bring your notebook from your secretarial room, which is the entrance to mine and from which you will be expected to shoo those boring souls I do not wish to see."

I brought my notebook—ready and waiting for me on the desk in the entrance room.

"I will dictate an editorial. I might say one of your main jobs will be to go around to the staff begging matches to keep my pipe going. Perhaps you'd better beg some now."

I rushed out to the city room and returned with matches. The city editor knew at once what I wanted. "Now, don't be afraid," he said. "Our Scot doesn't eat people."

Scot indeed! I had some Scotch in my ancestry myself and I could out-Scotch him in a fair tussle.

I returned with matches and notebook.

He put his feet on the desk, tamped his pipe, which I carefully lighted. He motioned me to a chair.

"Ready?" he asked.

"Yes sir."

"I shall dictate an editorial. Give the boy the copy to take down to the Linotype room and ask them to send up the proofs the minute they are done."

I had a Phi Beta Kappa key, which nothing in the world would make me wear, and when my diploma came by mail it had on it: "Graduated with great distinction," which both pleased and embarrassed me. But the moment my antique Scot began to dictate I knew that any day, possibly this one, my head was going to be lopped off at the neck.

He had the most marvelous vocabulary I had ever heard and he used every bit of it. When I went into my little office all I had were the easy little words, interspersed with huge holes. I filled in the holes as best I could and sent down the copy. Finally, when the proofs came up, the editor put his feet on the desk and began to read.

Once he looked up and said, "Did I say this?"

I said, "Well, sir, you said something quite like it."

Every morning before I went to work I went to shorthand school and spent three hours with an expert firing words at me to improve my shorthand, and every day I thought, "Today the ax will fall." This went on for three weeks. Then my ancient Scot announced calmly, "I am going to Del Monte to play in a golf tournament. I will be gone three weeks."

"And who will write the editorials and the column?" I asked.

"You will," he said firmly. "You are writing most of them anyway. By the way, what town did you say you came from?"

"Bellingham, sir. It's in the Cascades in the northwest corner of the country."

"Oh, yes, *Blingham*. I know it well. I will read your column while I am gone, and when I return I will line up the staff and permit each member one kiss for each mistake you have made."

Those three weeks were almost the death of me. I worked frantically on my shorthand. I looked up all the words except the "ands" and "buts."

One day the phone rang. It was my irascible Scot. He said, "You will be happy to hear I have found fourteen errors."

"No, you haven't," I said. "I looked up every word but 'and' and 'but.'"

"I trust the improvement will be permanent. The staff will be sorely disappointed. Beg some matches. I will be back tomorrow."

I had a small apartment, most of it sparsely furnished. When my work was done for the day I took the last streetcar, almost always empty except for myself and the motorman, who let me run the streetcar. We rattled happily through the night until the unexpected happened. He let me off. I had just started on the three-block walk, when a strange night person whose hands came down to his knees chased me home. The motorman, who usually waited to see that I got home safely, went after the night person. It was the first time in my life I had ever been so afraid. I had my key out, reached the apartment, opened the door, locked it and I sat on the stairs to collect myself. After this incident someone of the staff drove me home or I took a taxi.

One day E. K., as the staff called him behind his back, announced to me that he felt a short but serious attack of golf coming on.

"You notice I sign the front page 'Editor's Analysis' with my initials. Henceforth when I ask you to write it, you will sign it with your initials,

'M. C.' It will be your personal expression and yours alone."

About three times a week he asked me to write the column, and the first time it came out signed "M. C." I was up at dawn waiting for the paper to come so I could gaze upon it with rapture and trepidation. Oh, the thrill of it and the fear! It was my Scot who taught me the power of the written word.

At first I got us into alarming predicaments. I arrived at work one day to find the city editor waiting for me.

"Girl," he said, "go down to the Linotype room and stay there until I come for you. A young man from the water department has arrived and he swears if he finds you he is going to kill you."

The water department had dug a large hole in the street and neglected to light it. Hurrying to work in a heavy rain, I had fallen in.

"Is E. K. furious?" I asked the city editor when he came down for me.

"You underestimate him. He charmed the life out of the fellow. It is one of the things he does best. He said to me, 'I must say it is never dull around here with my young friend from *Blingham*. She gets us into the most amusing predicaments and I get us out.'"

Indeed! After that I took infinite care. I kept a large book of my successes and my blunders. The success section was called "Soft Sodder." The second section was called "Not So Soft." In one column I quoted Emerson thus: "On your despair you build your character." E. K. had me on the carpet at once. He had read the proofs.

"You're wrong," he said quietly. "It's 'On the debris of your despair you build your character.' Think about it. It's important."

One day, after twenty-five years as managing editor, my Scots benefactor was taken to the hospital with influenza and complications. He never returned. He was delirious and when the special night nurse went off to eat and rest, the younger nurses were afraid to be with him. His son and daughter could not handle him. She called me and I went out in a taxi. If he saw white whales with blue stripes, I saw blue whales with pink polka dots. We went on imaginary trips like small children playing a game.

One of the doctors I knew said to me, "Margaret, have you ever seen death?"

"No."

"Well, don't stay. It can be very tough at the end."

"I have to stay. Everything I have learned, he taught me."

The last night there was a change. He quieted and for a moment just before death he was completely lucid.

"I don't mind dying, Margaret," he said. "I've had a good life. You know something? You came into an old Scot's life like a benediction."

I called his son and the city editor, and left. I looked up the word "benediction" in the dictionary. "A blessing," it read.

I grieved for my friend. In the lead story, the city editor said E. K. had been born in Renfrew, Canada, set type in New York, returned to Renfrew and owned and operated his own newspaper there and later a paper in New Westminster, British Columbia. When it was virtually destroyed by fire, he had come to California and distinguished himself as a reporter on a San Francisco paper, helping to clean up the old Barbary Coast.

Had I ever really thanked him? I had not. I learned this then, to thank those who are good to you while they're alive to hear it. And I have never forgotten it.

The next editor was considerably older than E. K., a man of real distinction who had been the editor of several very noted papers. He did not write. I became his assistant at fifty dollars a week, which was a tremendous sum! He inherited me and treated me as formally as if I came from Mars.

Oddly enough, the people who most influenced me were several of my old professors whom I met by accident while I was working for the paper. One was my major professor, Payson Treat, a marvelous lecturer and an authority on Japanese history. He asked me what I was doing and I told him.

"There is something I must confess," I said shyly. "When I can't think of anything to write, I remember one of your lectures and I dish it up as closely as I can. The truth is, you are practically keeping me at least three days a week."

His eyes twinkled. "Good heavens, girl," he said, "if I had known that I'd have been charging you ten percent."

Another day I bumped into my favorite biologist. He spoke first. He said, "If I must lose a good biologist to scribbling, I expect to see her in *The Saturday Evening Post*. Do you hear me?"

I heard him. The time had come for action. The next day I knocked and went into the office of our new editor. My knees were wobbly.

"Please don't get up," I said. "I have a proposition to make and it's going to cause an explosion."

"It is, is it? Well, tell me. Don't stand there."

"I am never going to learn to write stories. There isn't time. I propose that you reduce my salary to twenty-five dollars a week and let me move to Palo Alto where I can write the column early in the morning and put it on the bus so it will be here by the time you arrive. Then I will have the rest of the day to try my hand at fiction."

The explosion was stupendous. You could hear it all over the building.

"You will starve to death. You will come back like Poe's cat."

"If I come back it will be in a pine box with a lily on top."

I won. The battle was long and noisy but I wore him down.

"You will never be any good until you get this ridiculous notion out of your head," he said at last. "When you come back your old job will be waiting for you."

This time I remembered to thank him. The office boy asked if he could kiss me good-bye, and he did.

Every morning I wrote the column and put it on the bus. Then I lay on the floor of the little duplex I had rented, surrounded by magazines, and I analyzed stories. For the first time I realized that professional creative writing is the only craft that must be practiced in silence and solitude. No happy chattering. No begging matches. I was alone. I had never known such loneliness, surrounded by an avalanche of crumpled yellow paper only good enough to end up on the floor.

One day I received a note from the woman who had given the English composition course to the students who had flunked "bonehead" English.

"It seems to me you will need a good agent. I enclose the address of one of the finest. Wait until you have a couple of stories that you think are the best you can do. Then send them. Tell him frankly that you are still writing the column. Good luck!"

I worked as I had never worked. Slowly I grew accustomed to loneliness. When I had two stories that were as good as I could do, I sent them with return postage. A letter came back that the agent liked my work very much; that he thought it would take about a year to work me into the large market; that he would like to see everything I wrote.

The Depression was upon us now. In books about the days of the stock market crash, it is the Conservation Corps, the Hooverville hobo jungles that are always mentioned. Nobody talks about the girls in the family who took care of destitute parents who had lost everything. No married woman could teach. If she married, she lost her job. If she worked in a bank and married, she was dismissed. It happened at Stanford even to the campus queens. It happened at Cal and at Mills. There was no Social Security. The poorhouse was unthinkable.

There are always some people so well-heeled they seem able to weather any catastrophe. There are always opportunists who find a way to run and leave others in the family to carry the load. I remember girl after girl who was not free to marry until she was thirty-eight or forty, or not at all. I remember one couple—the niece of a very famous writer (she taught until she was forty-two). The man she loved was burdened with his own parents and responsibilities. The country was still young. Integrity and courage had built it and integrity and courage pulled it through. The girls did not engage in self-pity or phony martyrdom. They did what they had to do. It was as simple as that.

There were still many magazines in which a young writer could start. These magazines were all edited by men, excellently trained, highly competent and completely ethical. It takes as much skill to make a fine editor as a writer. In the Depression raises were unknown and prices lower, but magazines still bought stories.

The *Delineator* bought my first story. Stephen Vincent Benét began there also. The magazine bought four or five of my stories a year, and it featured them thus: "This writer, young herself, puts into her work the delightful glow of youth." This filled me with horror. I would work myself to exhaustion and someone would say to me, "I read your *delightful little story* in the *Delineator*." I even killed off a few characters but the story came out "delightful and little" just the same.

Wilson was through law school now and found a job in a law firm in San Francisco. He met there a tall and pretty Stanford girl who was called north to help her widowed mother save valuable property near Lake Tahoe. He married her and moved to Sacramento to be near to help her mother.

Mother wrote that father had died. She said Wilson would be with her until everything was done and she advised me not to come home.

It was almost impossible to write and to recover from my grief; I took a month off and went to Colorado to visit my friend, Florence. She was a friend from Washington who had married Frank Means, a man with a forty-four thousand acre sheep ranch that had been in his family from the Spanish grant days.

Florence told me of Eleanor Quincy Adams

who had gone to Wyoming with her parents as guests of the governor and fallen in love with the governor's cowboy brother, the only man she had ever met totally unimpressed by her famous name. Frank, the sheep rancher, said she was so proud of her husband that when they went East to visit her family she insisted he wear his cowboy hat. At forty she had a child. Instead of going to Denver for the delivery, she went to a small railroad town and she and the baby died. Her husband was inconsolable. The Quincy Adams family sent him her share of the family jewels. Frank told me, "He still lives on the ranch she shared with him. Sometimes he brings me a fine ruby to hold for him until he can redeem it when his cattle are marketed. This is the way we trust each other here. You'll meet him. He'll ask us to drive up and see the ranch they shared. He'll probably let you ride her horse, which no one has ridden since her death three years ago, but I wouldn't try it if I were you."

I was a terrible disappointment. My bridge was atrocious. Florence insisted on trying to marry me off, but I realized Wilson and I had the responsibility of mother.

Frank showed me the circle in the grass where the Indians used to race their ponies, worn so deeply it was still visible. He picked up flint arrowheads beautifully made.

Mexicans helped with the ranch work and owned land also. One night Frank saw one of them sneaking up to change the valves on the water gates so Frank's water would go onto the Mexican's own land.

"Do you want to come along?" he asked me.

He took his rifle from the mantel and out we went into the deep night.

"This takes a really good shot," he said with a grin. "I wouldn't hurt him for the world, but I must come close enough so he will change those valves back in a hurry, otherwise none of us could live here."

The Mexicans trusted Frank. Once a Mexican boy beat his mother, and a large, irate Mexican delegation brought him to Frank. "We think he deserves to be punished. We ask you to beat him up." Frank beat him up.

The Mexicans went to school and some went on to college. They gradually acquired better water rights and built wooden houses instead of adobes. Some attained prominence in the state. It made our country seem suddenly very young.

One day Claude Sampson, Eleanor Quincy Adams' widower, arrived with a string of trout and at once asked us to visit his ranch they had shared, at Powderhorn. He asked me if I would like to ride his dead wife's horse. Declining, I chose a pleasantly docile looking beast that showed no inclination to stand up on his hind legs, pawing the air.

The ranch was atop a mesa, called a park, and the house was primitive, with none of the comforts his wife had known back East. Yet she had loved it and her husband also. I remember all went well until we came down off the mesa through the lovely quaking aspen which tradition says have been quivering since the death of Christ. It was so steep and the aspen so close together, everyone else could gauge the distance and swing one leg over the saddle horn. Not I! I barely managed to hang on and pray fervently not to be squashed.

When we got home, I could scarcely stand up.

Frank and his wife had lost a young son in an accident. They had three girls, the eldest away at an eastern school, and two small ones, Laura Belle and Frances, called Fina.

One day high in the tin-roofed corral we saw a rattlesnake chase a rat, moving at lightning speed—a familiar sight in Colorado.

An Indian girl was ironing clothes in the kitchen during a storm. A bolt of lightning hit the tin roof with a terrific explosion and a ball of fire rolled out of the iron and out of the kitchen, leaving the Indian girl in hysterics.

When Frank brought in a sick lamb, attacked by a coyote, dying because the coyote's paws were poisonous, Laura Belle was very upset. She took her best doll to place beside the lamb and comfort it.

After this series of frightening events, something strange happened to Laura Belle, who always looked so angelic. There was a change. There were some little half-grown chicks in the

yard. We found them one by one with their necks broken.

"Fina did it," said Laura Belle firmly, and Fina could not talk well enough yet to deny it.

Frank was away somewhere and I was too chicken myself to cut the chicks' heads off. I tried drowning them. That didn't work either.

"Fina did it," said Laura Belle firmly, but Fina had hurt her hand in the door and had it bandaged. By watching carefully we caught Laura Belle smacking the baby chicks on the head with a board.

Poor Florence! She took Laura Belle to her room and paddled her. The minute she left her, Laura Belle was out the window, smacking the young chicks with a board.

"I have raised a monster," Florence moaned.

When Frank returned he said "Nonsense. The rattlesnake chasing the rat scared her and then there was the lightning and ball of fire. Through hitting the chicks she found she too was bigger than something else."

He beheaded the bleating chicks. And I am glad to report Laura Belle outgrew her sense of power and turned into a perfect little lady.

I remember going on a picnic to a remote ranch high in the mountains. The men went off by themselves. There was a swift stream, not deep, running through the ranch. The women would let it carry them along. Since skinny-dipping was unheard of, the wife loaned us shirts so we would have dry clothes to wear home.

Florence said in the winter the husband took his wife traveling or she would develop melancholia because of the loneliness. Years later I saw this same thing at a place called Kingcome.

I loved Colorado. I loved the people who were so good to me and I have never forgotten any of them. I can see their faces, hear their voices and relive the funny things that happened. But I knew Colorado, too, was going to change. It was inevitable and it was sad.

After I returned from my month's vacation, my distinguished old editor, who had let me go to write with such protest and then done everything to help me, took sick and died.

A much younger man took his place. Whenever I wrote a really good column, off came my name and on went his.

It seems to me most people make relatively few important decisions. I made one now. I didn't even think about it. I marched into the publisher's office and I said, "If you wish to publish my work with no name at all, that's fine. But nobody's going to sign his name to what I write."

"But, Margaret," said the publisher, "if I tell him that, I am accusing him of stealing!"

"Isn't he?"

Three days later I was asked to turn in my typewriter. There was also a note from the new man. It read: "And when you write for *The Saturday Evening Post*, do come in to see us." I never did.

Youth looks ahead. I did not realize it, but I had followed in the path of most professional fiction writers of my day who leave the small town of little opportunity for a bigger challenge. Usually through long trial and error, they learn that the best they will write is not ahead, but back in their pasts.

I was to be lucky. Life was going to pick me up, turn me around and give me a painful push into that multisided perspective without which experience teaches us little of value.

Mother had now come to live with me.

One Sunday I took a bus to Berkeley to have lunch with an older professional friend who was going to drive me home. On the way the bus collided with a large flat truck. I was on the wrong side to see the accident coming and was thrown against the seat in front with a terrific wallop. Thirty-two people were sent to the hospital. When they came to me, the ambulances were all taken. A man taking his dog and his little boy for a ride drove me to the hospital. My friend found me there and drove me home.

At the local Palo Alto clinic the next day the doctor said, "You've broken your nose. It was a bit *retroussé*, which is a polite way of saying pug. Now it has a splendid hump. I think it's an improvement. You're from the North, aren't you? We will fatten you up, put you under a sunlamp and you'll be fine."

One day I bumped into the doctor after the sunlamp session and he asked me how my eyes were.

"No better."

"You might go to the city and see an ophthalmologist," and he gave me a name. "But my colleagues and I agree that any talk of a focal infection is nonsense. We have never seen one."

I went to the city and the minute the ophthalmologist looked into my eyes, he cleared the waiting room and called in the specialists. I had an absolutely clean bill of health, but this man was not one to give up. He brought in an expert who specialized in head X rays and he made large, very careful pictures of the broken nose.

"I can't be sure," he said "but there is something strange under the break, hidden, I think by two teeth. Let's have an extractionist pull them tomorrow."

I remember going back to Palo Alto that night utterly exhausted. Mother had a fire going and dinner ready.

"It doesn't look good," I said.

"It's going to come out all right," she said. "I know it."

The next day I went back to the city on the early train. The extractionist removed the two teeth, and the eye specialist attended. The pathologist found a staphylococcus and a microorganism he had seen only twice in a lifetime of work. I had missed losing both eyes by perhaps two weeks. The next day I could see twice as well.

I remember being deeply grateful for all the kindness they had shown me. I said, "When I think of all your combined efforts and goodness to me, I find it hard to excuse the doctor from Palo Alto who does not believe in focal infections."

They said gently, "An ophthalmologist sees them. He does not. Perhaps we have made a believer of him."

Mother and I moved to San Francisco into an old but pleasant eight-unit apartment on the edge of Russian Hill overlooking the bay. Once I went to Angel Island with a friend who worked there to watch the immigrants come in from Canton, China. Usually they came in with members of the diplomatic service, memorizing all they must know and throwing out the notes from a porthole before the boat landed.

The Chinese did not find white women attractive and the Chinese girls would be taken to Walnut Grove and sold into slavery. I went to the trial of the Chinese woman who had bought them for a few dollars in years of famine and whom the immigration authorities had been trying to catch for twenty years. She had the hardest, most evil face I had ever seen. She was dressed in a magnificent mink coat, pretended she could speak no English and answered only through an interpreter. This time they had caught her. It was an end to yellow slavery.

The unions had not changed the port as yet. I knew every boat that came in, those from Hawaii, from Japan, the Dollar ships that carried both passengers and freight.

Wilson had always brought home a gift to me, a piece of amber or once, a fat, squat wooden figure, a Buddha. The Chinese cleaning man who helped wash the windows saw it on the mantel and protested violently.

"Not for a woman," he said. "Very bad for a woman." He was so upset I asked him to take it away.

Now that we had settled in a place that we liked very much, we sent for the keepsakes stored with friends. And what a joy it was to see them again. There were two very old chairs with badly worn cane seats. When the Chinese cleaning man came again, I showed them to him.

"I bring friend to fix. I bring him tomorrow."

The next day he brought his friend who quoted an extremely modest price. He had brought a long, stout wand which he put over his shoulders with my precious old chairs hanging on the ends, and he said, "Three day, lady" and trotted off.

"Well," I thought, "there go my chairs. I don't even know his name. I'll probably never see them again."

I was wrong. In three days he was back, the chairs hanging on the rod, beautifully rubbed, polished and caned.

"You like?" he asked.

"I like. Thank you." And I bowed and he bowed also.

Then there was Frank Chung. During the school year he cooked in a fraternity house at Stanford. In the summer he worked at a Tahoe resort. Frank Chung had a wife and son in China. He had seen them once in twenty years. He had sent money to educate members of his family. Two were now doctors and Frank wished to become a citizen and to bring his son to live with him. He asked me if mother and I would be his witnesses in court and of course we said yes.

Now mother's family were of Scotch origin and to make a Scotch Presbyterian tell a whopper, especially in court, takes an act of God.

It scared Frank and me half to death. Mother went through it like a veteran.

The judge said, "Mrs. Craven, do you swear that you have seen Frank Chung three times a year for the past three years?"

"No," mother said calmly. "I have known him many years, but I cannot swear I have seen him so frequently."

The judge looked pained. Frank and I shook.

"All I can tell you, Judge," said mother "is that I have known Frank Chung a long time and I know him to be a man of complete integrity."

The act of God had occurred.

"Well," said the judge "I guess I can't ask for

anything better than that. Frank Chung, your citizenship is granted."

I remember Frank putting his arm around mother.

"Now," he said gently "we take grandma to lunch." And I could see the judge smiling.

Later Frank sent us a beautiful Chinese vase on a teakwood stand. I still cherish it.

A friend of mine who had grown up in San Francisco with Alice B. Toklas asked me if I would like to meet Gertrude Stein, who was arriving soon for a visit.

"No, indeed," I replied. "I wouldn't have the slightest idea what she was talking about."

Nevertheless, the phone rang the next day and Alice B. Toklas said, "Gertrude Stein is expecting to see you at the Mark Hopkins hotel at ten o'clock tomorrow morning."

I said that I considered this an imposition and not for the world would I take up Miss Stein's time. It did no good. The next morning I went to the hotel, feeling young and very scared.

There were newspaper men and photogr
phers all around the desk. When I gave my nam
the clerk said, "Oh, yes, Miss Craven, go right u
Miss Stein is expecting you."

Alice B. Toklas ushered me in and went out
meek as a small mouse.

Miss Stein was propped up in bed, wearing a
red velvet robe, writing letters. She put down her
letters.

She said, "Come, sit on the bed."

I chose a far corner.

"Now, what do you want to talk about?"

Sink or swim. Do or die!

"Well," I said, "I don't want to ask you what
you mean by your work. I know what it means to
me and that is my business."

I stayed about three hours and never had a
better time. No one was ever nicer to me. I do not
remember what I said, but I have not forgotten
Miss Stein's vital eyes, face, voice. All the way
home on the cable car I wrote down her words:

"Every writer must have common sense. He
must be sensitive and serious. But he must not
grow solemn. He must not listen to himself. If he
does, he might as well be under a tombstone.
When he takes himself solemnly, he has no more
to say. Yet he must despise nothing, not even

solemn people. They are part of life and it's his job to write about life.

"Be direct. Indirectness ruins good writing. There is inner confusion in the world today and because of it people are turning back to old standards like children to their mothers. This makes indirect writing.

"A writer must preserve a balance between sensitivity and vitality. Highbrow writers are sensitive but not vital. Commercial writers are vital but not sensitive. Trying to keep this balance is always hard. It is the whole job of living.

"When one writes a thing—when you discover and then put it down, which is the essence of discovering it—one is done with it. What people get out of it is none of the writer's business.

"Every writer is self-conscious. It's one reason he is a writer. And he is lonely. If you know three writers in a lifetime, that is a great many.

"You do not have to write what the editors want. You can write what you want and if you develop sufficient craftsmanship, you can sell it, too. I want you to write for *The Saturday Evening Post*. It demands the best craftsmanship."

One thing more. Miss Stein discussed Ernest Hemingway, the sensitive young man with a lovely wife and the baby "Bambi." She spoke objectively, with a touch of sadness, about the change that had come with *The Sun Also Rises*, and the beginning of his egomania. Much later when he died and his official biography came out, I realized she knew whereof she spoke.

She asked me to write her. I never did. I was too shy.

When the Second World War came, I had overcome my "delightful little story" complex. The country was suddenly prosperous with all our many-sided talents hurrying supplies to Europe. When we were in the war and the wounded were coming home, I was writing for all the big markets except *McCall's*, *Pictorial Review* and *Cosmopolitan*. The *Post* had said to my agent: "We could be buying now, but we want her best. We want that number one story, and she is capable of it."

The *Post* began to buy my short stories in 1941.

One of the finest publishers had asked to do my first book.

One day I realized I could see nothing with

my left eye and I went at once to the ophthalmologist who had found the bacterium and staphylococcus.

"The left eye has a cataract forming. We expected it, but we didn't tell you. We thought you'd had enough, but here in San Francisco we have the finest specialist on cataracts. He will remove it and the left eye will get you by when the right eye fails."

"How long will that be?"

"A very long time probably. In old people the two would come close together, but you're not old. It could be many years."

"I won't be able to write books, will I?"

"I doubt it," he said, "but I am willing to bet you will do some splendid stories."

By day I was brave as a lion, but the nights were terrible. I remember one night when a comet tail filled the sky with tiny glowing particles and I saw it from our big window in the apartment which overlooked the bay, and I said, "Other people do things as hard as this. I am people, and I can."

The next morning something very strange happened. The phone rang and it was a wounded lieutenant from Letterman, the military hospital.

"I am Lieutenant Evan Hill. I don't know

you. I don't know anyone who does know you. There are several of us here interested in writing. We read somewhere that you lived here and hoped you might come and talk to us."

The date had been set for the operation and I told him about it.

"Do you have someone who could drive you here?" he asked slowly.

I said, "The woman next door drives for the Red Cross and I am sure she would."

"Come tomorrow about three o'clock," he said, and he gave me the ward number.

"Don't worry about finding us. We will find you."

Oh, my blessed infantry. What would I ever have done without you? They were waiting for me all smiles and jokes and laughter.

"We have each other, but you are alone. We need you and you need us. We are adopting you."

And adopt me they did. I will never forget that afternoon.

There was one with a cast from his waist to his feet, who would always be lame. There was another, wounded by shrapnel that had not hit his eyes at all but damaged the part of his brain that receives the images of sight. He had had a brilliant political future ahead of him. Now he had tunnel vision, a narrow slit of sight, clear but pencillike, and he could not go anywhere alone without getting lost. I remember the ward nurse with a huge laundry bag on wheels. When she told them to quiet down, they dumped her into the bag, feet sticking out, sputtering loudly.

They asked about my operation. I knew they knew exactly what it meant.

"Why, it will only take a bit more than an hour. Here we don't even count them unless they take five hours, which is about our average."

When I left I said, "I will be back as soon as I can."

They laughed and said, "You haven't taught us to write yet. What we should do is keep you here. You won't be able to see us and we could put a screen around you and hide you from the brigadier."

Already I had changed. I could think of my father without pain and the lovely summers in the mountains during my youth. I could remember asking him what was gallantry, and he had answered that gallantry was missing part of life that most people take for granted, to know you couldn't have it back and to take it not only with courage, but with grace. "It is an unforgettable thing to see," he had said.

When they operated on my left eye at the old Stanford Hospital in San Francisco, they did it with a local anesthetic, and I did exactly as I was told: "Look down, look right, keep absolutely still." I was packed in sandbags, with private nurses around the clock and with orders to let no one kiss me or even touch the bed.

I remember Wilson and mother came in briefly. The last day, when I was to go home—the stitches out, my eyes still bandaged—the head nurse, an old army veteran, came in.

"The whole infantry has arrived," she said dryly. "At least they are making that much noise. Do you want to see them?"

Did I? I didn't really see them, of course, but I knew their voices. The one on crutches with a cast from his waist to his heels was draped over the end of the bed. He was Evan Hill. The one with tunnel vision was Jim Grimsley. They were full of talk and laughter and told me all the funny things that had happened in the ward.

"I will be over to see you as soon as I can," I promised.

"We will be waiting for you. You are never going to get away from us."

I never did. When they had gone the head nurse came back.

"Do you like them?" I asked her.

"I love them. If I had never known boys like them I would feel I had missed the best part of my life."

When I was able to go over to see my infantry we talked writing. They were mother hens looking out for a wayward chick.

"Orders," they said. "When you walk behind anybody, he will have four feet; two bright ones— that's your better eye—and two dim ones. That's your dim eye. We had a boy in here with an artificial leg and some idiot took him on a binge to celebrate before he was ready and scared him nearly to death. The Doc says you will get used to it, but it will take time. No accidents! Understand?"

I promised.

One day a man from the apartment drove me over to see them and I made the introductions.

"This is Lieutenant Evan Hill and this is Lieutenant Jim Grimsley, and this—"

"Why, Margaret," the man said, "they're all captains."

"What? How long has this been going on?"

"About six weeks. We thought we would wait to see how long it took you to notice it."

"You know I can't tell a general from a majordomo. It's villainy. That's what it is."

"And by the way, Margaret," Evan said, "the *Post* no longer costs a nickel."

When I thought I could do it, I asked them to dinner and I let them choose the menu. They wanted steak and lemon meringue pie.

The pie took me from eight in the morning until half past four. The whites of the eggs were all double and kept disappearing in some mysterious way.

By noon I was licked. I lay down, trying to feel sorry for myself, growing madder and madder. I got up and went to the store. I had to cross a street with very heavy traffic. By some luck I got across and bought another dozen eggs. I started back. The traffic was worse. A little Italian girl was waiting, also.

"Come on," I said, "they can't run over both of us."

"Gee, I'm glad you happened along. I've just had a corneal transplant."

"I've just had a cataract operation."

We both laughed.

"Tell me something," she said. "When you pour his coffee, do you pour it in your husband's lap?"

"No, but I would if I had one."

When I reached home I numbered the bowls in which the eggs were separated. Michelangelo himself painting the Sistine Chapel could have been no more careful.

We had a splendid time. I might say I have never made another lemon meringue pie in my life. When a girl is ahead, she'd better have brains enough to stay there.

I didn't mind not doing a book. I liked stories and the *Post* was always wonderful to me. Just once I used some of the things my blessed infantry had taught me in a story. The *Post* senior editor, Erd Brandt, came out every other year or so to see what his writers were doing. I was asked to dinner.

"Well, Margaret, what are you up to?"

"If I tell you, you will spill the coffee on the table and say 'Good heavens, you can't write that!'"

"How do you know?"

"I don't know. I just have a writer's hunch. I just have one chance to please you and I'm not going to risk it. Slice me up in little pieces but tell you I will not."

"Well," he said thoughtfully "you may be right."

When I sent the story in I received back a telegram.

"We have an unbreakable rule never to put wounded men into our fiction. But you have done such a beautiful job we are making one exception. Congratulations from us all. As ever thine, Erd."

I have never lost my blessed infantry, and other wounded have increased their number. One by one they went their way, but not until I had met their wives, or girls they later married.

Jim Grimsley sells real estate in Van Nuys and his wife helps him.

Evan Hill was the last to go. He completed his education and became head of the journalism department at the University of Connecticut. He has written books and good ones.

Evan said to me, "If I ever get up there I shall say to the Man Upstairs 'there are some things I don't like on your earth.'"

And I answered, "I am older than you are and I'll drag you in if it's the last thing I do."

Evan said, "I can just see you. There will be a great bright sign in the sky 'Craven's Pie Works' and under it a smaller sign 'Heavenly Pies.'"

I hear from my infantry yearly.

The last story I wrote for the *Post* before my second operation was about a Basque sheep herder. The circle of sight with the better eye, which was almost operable, had grown so small I could not recognize anyone outside of nine feet. When I went to Dixon to watch a man work his sheep, I took along a friend to help me.

"What's he doing now?" and she would describe it carefully.

When I sent it to the *Post* I scrambled the heading by hitting the wrong typewriter keys. The young man who wrote the "Keeping Posted" page wrote back and said, "What does this mean? I can't read it."

I have always been a little ashamed of myself.

"If you don't know, ask Erd." And I signed it "I write 'em, you read 'em, Craven."

When the second eye was operable—Wilson's marriage had failed and he was alone. As the population grew and the need for city apartments increased, rents went up and heat went down, and since the steep hills of San Francisco were too much for mother now, Wilson and I bought a house in Sacramento where we could be together and mother could get outdoors.

Wilson took me to San Francisco when it was time to operate on the eye. But with what a difference! No sandbags. It was done under a general anesthetic and went so well I was sure to come out with better sight than I had had for years.

When my wonderful new glasses came I would get up at dawn because strong sunlight was too bright. I would go outdoors, fascinated by the pattern of the roof across the street, the blades of grass, the color of the flowers, the brush marks on the house next door. Nothing else mattered. I turned out a poor story and another. It didn't bother me at all.

When I finally got downtown, my brother said to me, "Margaret, take that horrible smile off your face. You have just beamed at the worst pimp in this town and what's more he beamed right back."

One day the phone rang. It was Erd Brandt. Speaking to him was like being smacked in the face by an old dead mackerel. What was the matter with me? He knew I wasn't lazy. That was the only night in my life I didn't sleep a wink. I know only four swear words which I believe can be put into sixteen combinations. I invented some new ones.

"You great big conceited so-and-so. You long-legged this and that!"

In the morning the phone rang. It was Erd-man and he wanted the telephone number of some writer in San Francisco. Could I give it to him? I did so.

"And how are you?" he asked slowly.

"How am I? Well, I'll tell you how I am. I feel just like a hen ordered back to the nest to lay nothing but double-yolked eggs." I threw it at him—kerplunk!

"That's right," he said complacently. "That's exactly right. Good-bye."

I failed one more story and then I wrote a good one. A telegram came back: "You're back on the beam. Congratulations from us all."

Some months later Erd's son, flying a new experimental airplane, disappeared with his plane. A search was made over three states and no trace was ever found. I wrote Erd a note, of course, and he wrote back.

"Margaret, you never complained once. You never lost your sense of humor, your love of laughter, your independence. I find in you now a tower of strength."

One of the last stories I wrote for the *Post* was based on the experience of an Episcopal minister who, as a young man from England, had worked at Masset in an Indian village in the Queen Charlotte Islands. Wilson had been up the Inside Passage and stopped at the Queen Charlotte.

"I think there's a story there," Wilson said, "and I asked my friend if he'd talk to you. He said he would."

For the first time in my life I was going to write a story on material I knew nothing about and had not seen myself. I did this very carefully.

When the story "Indian Outpost" was published, I received many letters about it, especially from Canada. One was from the captain of the hospital ship that patrolled the inlets. He asked if I would like to know his ship "since I knew the country so well." He sent me the *Log* published several times a year by the Columbia Coast Mission. The newsletter was filled with bits of happenings of inside inlets of which I had never heard. There was one brief item about an old chief who was giving a large potlatch in anticipation of his death, at a remote village called Kingcome. I had that strange feeling an old professional feels when, usually after long search, he collides with material he recognizes somehow as his own. Here

I was! I not only saw well again after many years of waiting, I could write a book at a time when the fine old magazines were folding one by one, not because the subscribers had turned to television, but because the cost of mailing had risen from four million a year to twenty-eight million a year, to forty-eight million a year, to fifty-eight million a year and higher and higher. Soon there would be no market for the creative writer, though no one yet believed it could possibly affect the *Post*.

I thought about it very carefully. I went to the state library and read everything I could find about the inlets on the west coast of Canada, even about the flora and the animals. Franz Boas, an American anthropologist, began his work there and other anthropologists had followed him. I did not want to go as an authority on native culture. I wrote down only a few things that impressed me with their beauty. Then I wrote the Columbia Coast Mission, told them of my story in the *Post* and my years of work there and asked if I might come up and talk to some of the young Anglican priests who had worked in the Indian villages. I did not ask to go to Kingcome—wherever it was. That would have seemed to me to be presumptuous.

I received a letter that said they knew of my Indian story in the *Post* and liked it because it was not sentimental. They were referring my letter to Eric Powell, their authority on Indian villages, from whom I would hear.

Eric Powell wrote that he would expect me in Powell River in September and named the date.

"I am vicar of the church in this paper mill town and fly to Kingcome each month. The boat stationed at Kingcome is in Vancouver for its annual overhauling. I will send you to Kingcome when the boat comes. You must see it. Meanwhile, you can stay at the small hotel and have your dinners here at the vicarage. I have several Indian boys living with me who are working in the pulp mill here preparatory to working their way through college. This will give you a chance to know the Indians gradually."

Most of the passengers got off at Seattle. At Vancouver the immigrants were taken off first. None had been permitted to get off the plane in the States. One was a Chinese, I think from Red

China, who spoke excellent English and was on his way to Edmonton to study medicine. I sat next to him. I remember trying my best to be friendly. Though he was polite, it was obvious he wanted nothing to do with Americans. When the plane landed, the customs man rushed out to take off the immigrants. There was a Chinese couple, Cantonese, beautifully dressed, obviously of the diplomatic corps. There was also a little old Chinese woman in a thin dress. When the customs man drew near her, she would not budge. The diplomatic corps disdainfully offered no help and the customs man looked desperately at me.

"Will you help me? I will go ahead and bring back an interpreter."

"I will try."

I put my arm around her, knowing she couldn't understand a word I said.

"Don't be afraid. I won't let anyone harm you," and she looked at me carefully and off we went. The customs man came running out with the interpreter.

"I don't know what I would have done if you hadn't helped me," he said, and when I waited my own turn to go through customs, the Red Chinese medical student was all smiles.

"Now remember what I told you," I said to

him. "Play a little. My brother and I worked too hard. You will make a fine doctor and your country will be proud of you."

"I will remember and I thank you."

To my dismay, the airstrip at Powell River was being resurfaced. I was going to be three hours late. I sat where the small plane which was to take me to the pulp mill town to meet Eric Powell would land. I watched the plane come in from Prince Rupert with fishermen, their children and grandchildren meeting them with joy. Then at last a small plane came and I got on it. When it landed, there was Eric Powell in his clerical collar.

I said, "I was determined not to be one bit of trouble and the first thing I do is arrive three hours late."

The people around Eric all laughed and he said, "We will drop your luggage at the hotel. Then we will drive to the vicarage. The Indian boys who live with me are getting your dinner."

In the vicarage there was one beautifully carved small totem, a chief's carved serpent stick and a lovely mask, all gifts evidently. There was a small and very ancient bowl to hold the chief's spittle and a large and ancient carved canoe paddle.

The Indian boys watched me very carefully and quietly. There is one way to all boys' hearts, sure and reliable, and I knew it well. Dive into the dishwater with them. When they wash, you dry and when they dry, you wash.

When I returned to my hotel, I found, out of sight on its lower floor, there was a beer parlor. The loggers in from some far camp with money in their pockets and no wives to greet them were very, very drunk. The Mounted Police arrived. I did not dare stick my head out the second floor window for fear of being conked with a bottle.

While we waited for the boat to come from its overhauling, I found myself making a bit of progress.

"Do you remember if your grandfather ever called the salmon the 'swimmer' and the halibut 'the old woman'?"

The boys said, "Yes, but how did you know?"

I would get out some fragment of the research I had written down and read it aloud. Where there is no written language, much is lost over the long years. The ancient language is unknown to the young, and the words change their meaning. These boys were as eager to know more of their own history as I was.

I remember that Ernest Willie, one of the Indian boys who worked in the pulp mills preparatory to going to college, felt that when the Indian Affairs Department forbade the elaborate ancient dances, it was as if the tribe had lost what was as important as our inauguration. He told me that a version of the famous cannibal dance was permitted.

Eric laughed and said to Ernest Willie, "When you were a small boy you danced the *hamatsa* dance and now it is likely you will be the first Anglican priest from the village to represent your Indian peoples in Toronto"—which Ernest did.

Eric Powell was in his mid-thirties. Working his way through college, he had broken his back in a logging accident. His condition was inoperable and there was danger that eventually his spine would fuse and confine him to a wheelchair. He seldom mentioned it. He was like my infantry, full of laughter and of joy. He swallowed pain pills. When the vibrations of the boat became too painful, the doctor kept him in Powell River. Then he would fly up to the settlements in a tiny seaplane once a month to give communion, to marry, to confirm, to bury. He was grateful for the health he had. He loved and understood the Indians. He had not married and would not.

In the evenings, when the boys left to work in the pulp mill, Eric would tell me of his first days at Kingcome, his back less painful then. How dumb he was. How little he knew. How long it had taken him to know the Indians.

"When they laugh with you, you have made progress. When they come to laugh at you, you know they are beginning to let you inside the mystery, but it is when you suffer with them that the door really opens."

I would make notes of all I had seen and learned that day, after he had taken me back to the hotel.

It was very rough when the *John Antle*, the boat stationed at Kingcome, arrived from its overhauling. Eric insisted that the boat continue to Lund, protected by Cortes and Redonda Islands. We would travel by car as far as the road went.

"I don't want Miss Craven to start her trip seasick," he said, piling me and the boys into a car. When we arrived in Lund and I saw what I was up against, I had an unholy desire to annihilate the woman who had sold me my ticket north.

"Now don't wear slacks. Americans always think because it is Canada, they can slop around in slacks. Surprise them."

I did indeed! I had on a red wool suit with a fairly tight skirt, a gray topcoat with a red lining, a small red velvet hat with a veil.

When the *John Antle* arrived at a small marina, Eric introduced me to Ron Dean and his wife, Dorothy, and to a young white man, Douglas Embree, from Vancouver, who was acting as deckhand. On the aft deck was an organ a church was sending to Kingcome. It took up the entire deck. There was no gangplank. The only way onto that boat was to climb up the bow, one toe in a porthole at a time.

Thank heavens I had bought some warm wool panties at the Hudson's Bay store and a pair of large red flats. Several days earlier, friends of Eric's had asked me to dinner. A bear walked into the yard to steal some apples. I had not expected to be chased by bears, and decided then that I needed shoes that would allow me some mobility. The red flats certainly made my boarding the *John Antle* less hazardous.

I began to climb. When I managed to clamber aboard, there they stood, Eric and his boys. The boys had to return to Powell River where they would have to work all night at the pulp mill. There was a strange look on Eric's face. The Indians' sad eyes were filled with laughter, but not one drop spilled over. They waved. I waved. The adventure had begun.

When we approached the Yuculta Rapids, Ron said, "We are a bit late for the ebb tide, but this boat is strong enough to make it." And he fixed me a stool to sit beside him at the left of the wheel. "On the other side we will pass many boats waiting for tomorrow's ebb and we will pass tugs coming with large booms of logs that cannot get through today. I want to be well beyond them so we can get an early start in the morning."

"Where is Dorothy?" I asked.

"She doesn't like to go through the rapids and is in the galley baking something special for dinner."

Ron got out a chart and on it he sketched our route. I remember those rapids and the pools of deep swirling waters and the skill with which he took us through them. When we were through at last, I remember the boats waiting for tomorrow's ebb. When we passed a tug slowly hauling a boom of logs, a hand waved from the open cabin door and we waved back.

Finally, after passing all the anchored boats, we tied up at Shoal Bay in the silence, in the quiet and the loneliness.

There was a straight drop to the galley. Ron and Dorothy went up and down, agile as monkeys. I went slow as a sloth, faced the wrong way, barking my shins and praying I wouldn't break my neck.

"When we come to a float store, we are going to buy you some slacks," Ron said firmly. "If I let you break an arm or leg, Eric will never forgive me."

The next day we went up a bit of the Johnstone Channel, through a scattered school of killer whales. They watched us. Some were thirty feet long. They waited until we were close to them and at the very last minute, sounded and went down. Dot said she and Ron had been fishing one day in the Kingcome Inlet when a school of killer

whales had herded salmon to the river that runs by the village, where fish go up to spawn, as a dog herds sheep. The killer whales were leaping over their boats. Sometimes the whales came down flat on the water with a terrific boom to knock off the barnacles.

We turned off Johnstone Strait into one of the inlets and tied up at what remained of an ancient village, deserted and utterly still. The next day we started early and stopped at Simoon Sound at a store moored to an island.

"Now don't forget those slacks," Ron said. "This is our last chance. Dorothy, you stock up on groceries. I will check the oil and the propane and the kerosene."

I was so happy and pleased that I was about to purchase slacks that I dropped off the boat—slid off the bow and walked along humming.

"No humming is permitted on this island." And I looked at Dorothy conducting herself like a perfect lady and I tried desperately not to smile.

"Absolutely no humming is permitted on this island."

I went into the float store and asked the man in charge if he had slacks: two pairs, lined; one black and one plaid.

"Here they are. Just pull this curtain around

you and try them on. Three-ninety each, the very best."

There were two loggers in from months in some far camp, money in their pockets. They were very, very drunk.

"Oh, we will help her," said the two drunks eagerly.

"No, you won't," said the proprietor. "Now stop that."

There was a loud, prolonged scuffle.

I held up the two pairs of slacks. The black ones looked about right. I grabbed them, gave the man the money and bolted. I went up the bow of the boat while he was still wrestling with the drunks.

In my cabin, off with the skirt, on with the slacks. A mother raccoon and her babies were outside the first porthole, holding up their little hands, making queer whirring noises and begging for food. I opened the porthole and fed them.

I sat as usual at Ron's left. At night we traveled always with a spotlight, watching for deadend logs that float end up and can take the bottom out of your boat. I liked watching the fish in the phosphorescence off the bow. I had no idea the birds fished all night, the gulls waiting until the boat was almost upon them to lift, only to drop the instant it had passed. When Ron blew the whistle they rose and came down as one. Ron seemed very content. He took his hands off the wheel and began to sing, making some very strange movements in the air.

"What in the world are you doing?" I asked.

"I am drawing a picture of you in those delightful slacks."

Where we tied up that night I do not know. Somewhere near the float store I suppose. I had become a perpetual note taker. I scribbled notes in the dark, sitting beside Ron on the night run, the fish flashing, the gulls lifting. I would awaken at night and remember something I had forgotten to write down and reach in the dark for the ever-present pencil.

I remember well when we went through Panphrey's Pass which led us into the twenty-three mile inlet of Kingcome.

Ron was very quiet. We slipped through one pass so narrow I thought the boat would never get through without scraping a huge rock covered with seaweed.

"The Indians call it Whale Pass," Ron said. "They believe the gods turned a whale into this rock. Sometimes a dolphin races us here. I will never get used to it. I always feel I have come to the end of the world."

We moved into the inlet in the rain. There was nothing but silence and the great mountains. On the far side of the inlet, where lightning had struck a tree, there was a strip of bare granite where the slide had peeled off every bit of soil. It looked like a scar left by a huge grizzly and I could see small falls tumbling over the cliff. We tied up on the inside of the government float, where there would be no roll, one-third mile from the end of the inlet.

"In the morning I'll lower the speed boat and take you, Dorothy, Doug, and all the luggage, food and gear to the village. The electricity will be off. It always is when we are away. Somebody can't resist tinkering with the generator. We have lights only in the vicarage and the church. This is the only electricity in the village and it is off at night. Then tomorrow I'll return with some Indian boys and two thirty-foot canoes, and we will bring in the organ."

I could see painted across the cliff a long line of sheep, cattle, goats, coppers which Ron said marked the gifts of a great potlatch.

"Very old?" I asked.

"Nineteen thirty-six. In the morning you will see the hand of the welcome totem among the trees."

We were up early. Ron checked the bilge, an important chore he said, because the boat could catch fire if a man were too busy to do it. We washed the dishes, placed them behind the little racks that held them tight in a gale, checked the log, put away the chart, cleaned the refrigerator, closed the portholes and made the beds. We all helped. After putting on their gum boots, Ron and Doug loaded us into the speedboat with all the supplies. I saw the hand of the welcome totem.

When we reached the channel where the river entered the village, there were logjams in shallow water. Ron said, "In the winter this is unbelievable. The wind can blow the mailbags right out of the boat. It freezes you to the bone. Sometimes it is so shallow you have to get out and drag the canoes."

When we entered the river, Ron pointed out Whoop-Szo, the noisy mountain, so named because of the many slides on it. We pulled up in front of the vicarage, and for the first time I saw the church of Saint George. There were white alders edging the bank. I heard the raven and I saw two bald eagles soaring the skies.

"I have strict orders to carry you ashore," Ron said.

"Never, not me." Ron laid some boards to the

beach which I walked while Doug and Ron waded and helped me. Though the generator was off when we reached the vicarage, a fresh loaf of bread, still warm from the oven, was on the kitchen table.

"They knew we were coming. They almost always do, but how?" Ron asked.

Dorothy made some hot coffee. Ron returned to the boat with the Indian boys and the canoes to bring back the organ.

When we left the house and stepped outside, no one was visible. It was Saturday and even the smaller children, not old enough to go to the government school at Alert Bay, were nowhere to be seen. Doug Embree called them, using their Indian names, and out they came rushing to meet him. Doug introduced me.

"Margaret is a friend of Eric's," he reassured them. "He wants us to be good to her."

When we returned to the village, a little boy and girl were waiting. They touched nothing. They did not speak.

"Would you like to show Margaret the village?" Dorothy asked, and they nodded eagerly. The little boy ran ahead to show me how he could go up the greased pole that stood by the big totem in front of the church. The little girl said, "I love the snow on the mountaintop." I thought of how many times I had said the same words when looking at the snow on the Cascades in my youth.

Now the Indians had been reassured and were going about their chores. I remember the little girl and me holding hands at the river's edge and watching an old Indian woman paddle out and drop her garbage in the salt chuck or water. We strolled through the village and I saw T. P. Wallace, the orator, the only man left whose head had been bound as a baby, with tight thongs to widen it. He would have been perfectly at home among the ancient Roman bronzes.

I saw Mr. Green who was totally deaf. He was always called Mr. Green. He was immaculate in neat trousers, white shirt and tie. What did he think in his soundless world, of the white woman who had come here?

I saw a husband and wife outdoors doing the family washing, the man helping his wife, the ancient washer using kerosene for fuel. I saw the great totem that stood by the church.

Ron returned in time for dinner and the Indians with him lifted the organ from the canoes and carried it into the church.

"Won't play a note," Ron said. "I am afraid the rain didn't help any, but it will dry out in time.

Now I must fix the generator or we will have no lights. Make dinner a bit late, Dorothy."

That night I had what to me was an horrific experience. In the middle of the night I was aware I was sharing the bed with something that moved. Ron had fixed the generator, but at night the lights in the vicarage were turned off as always. You were on your own with a flashlight. I got up, checked to be sure the door was closed so I wouldn't wake up the whole house. I turned back the bed. There was the biggest spider I had ever seen. Including its legs, of which it seemed to have an abundance, it must have measured five inches across. Clutching the flashlight, I grabbed the wool panties I had bought at Powell River, dropped them over the spider and assaulted it with a shoe.

In the morning I was up first. I disposed of what was left of the spider in the bathroom, washed out the panties, put them on a hanger and hid them in my closet.

"Margaret," Ron said, "why in the world were you up so early?"

"Disposing of an absolutely immense spider."

"Did you hear that, Dorothy? She didn't know it was harmless, but she killed it anyway and all by herself. I will introduce her at church as assaulting a poor spider who was looking for a warm and free bed. They will love it."

"No, you won't," I said firmly. "I'll tell them myself, but not at church."

Ron Dean could not give communion. He had been divorced. Today he could be admitted to the clergy, but not then. An Englishman, he told fascinating stories of the war, when he had even played in a band accompanying the troops and entertaining them. He could tell the best ghost stories in all this world. At school he had been caned for so many pranks that he must have been the despair of his father who lived at Brighton. In all my life I have never heard the Anglican service more beautifully spoken. Every word held its unforgettable and perfect quality. I think he liked Evensong best. He asked me then, to stand beside him. I watched the Indians coming with their lanterns up the path from the far end of the village. Ron introduced me as they entered, always with some personal word. "She is Eric's friend and he wants us to help her. She is not an anthropologist. She is interested in you and I shall ask you to come to the vicarage so she can come to know you and understand you."

I could not, of course, pronounce an Indian word.

"Ron," I would say with great seriousness, "would you mind telling me the name of this village?"

And Ron would say slowly, "These are the Kwakiutl Indians and the village is called Tsawa-taineuk," and to save my life I could not tell whether he said "Jowedaino" or "Zowodaino" or "Chowudaino."

"I am absolutely sunk," I moaned. "Here I am ready to write a book I thought I would never be able to write and I can't even pronounce the tribe's name."

"Oh, I haven't given you the real humdinger, the name of the cannibal who lived at the north end of the world."

"It can't be any worse."

It was. It was Bakbakwalanuksiwae.

"Spell it," I said.

"I can't. If it makes you feel any better, nobody, but nobody can spell it."

Sometimes I walked into the church of Saint George all by myself looking at the hand-carved altar, the great carved golden eagle, which was the lectern, its talons close together, the head turned to look proudly down at its feet, its wings parted to hold the Bible. I saw the carved chair where the "Bissop," as the children called him, sat, and a lovely life-sized painting of Christ holding a little lamb. Painted by one of the Indians of real talent, Christ's face was an Indian face with an Indian's sad eyes. On the way out I poked an organ key. It did not answer.

One day Dorothy and I decorated the church with fishnets and in the nets we put fish cut from colored papers. Why, I am not sure.

The women of the village, as in all churches, had a guild. They crocheted beautiful table runners and made baskets and lovely shawls. Since there was no one else to buy them, they sold them to each other to raise their donations.

One day Ron told me about old Peter, the carver, and some of the elders of the village coming to ask his help. T. P., the orator, spoke for them since some were so old they spoke only the ancient Kwakwala. Long ago the burial ritual of the Indians involved placing their dead in a square box and hanging the box on a large tree, the lower limbs cut off so no animals could reach the coffin. Each family had its burial tree. The boxes had fallen and the old carvings and totems which stood on the ground below each family's tree had disintegrated with age and were beyond repair. The Indians asked Ron to help build a communal grave so they would know at last the bones of their ancestors were at peace.

With Eric's agreement, Ron had rounded up younger Indians to help him and for days they lowered the boxes and the broken totems and placed them in a huge communal grave. Some of the mummified hands still wore copper bracelets, paper thin. They also buried their own clothes. When Eric came, he held a brief service on the huge communal grave.

An old Indian said, "At last a man has come to us who saw to it that our dead can rest in peace."

I asked Ron, "In the old, old days the terrible cannibal dance, the *hamatsa*, and the supernatural myths and magic were all fake, weren't they?"

"Yes. Peter, who lived at the end of the village, knew that but his great-grandparents did not. It was very serious. If a man moved in the dances when he heard the hamatsa coming, he was killed. No one alive has ever seen the days when a body was taken from a grave tree and the hamatsa and cannibal dancer pretended to take a bite from the body. But I am glad the memories of witchcraft and the supernatural are at rest. And after all, just remember my country had its ghost stories and yours its Salem witches."

Once a plane broke the sonic barrier. The boom was caught in the inlet and bounced from one steep mountainside to another, the sound very loud and lasting a long time. The children were excited. The adult Indians ignored it.

Once a helicopter came to pick up two Indians who were logging in some distant camp and the pilot took the children for a ride around the village—to their delight.

Once, just once, I saw an animal shot. The Indians did not shoot for fun, only for necessity. A timber wolf was molesting the village. It weighed one hundred fifty pounds and the women were afraid it would carry off a small child in its big hideous teeth.

I never saw a child spanked or slapped. I never saw an impudent or rude child. The children were always wonderful to me, but the Indians I liked most of all were the young women. They were gentle, but strong. I remember one who had been sent to the hospital at Alert Bay with TB. The nurses called her the "little princess" and a princess she was. There were several of the girls from the prominent old families, all attractive, with a gentle, charming appeal. In Hawaii you could scarcely have told them from the natives.

It was fall now, and cold. The boat had not been out of the village, so no mail had gone. One night there was a terrible storm. It passed over the village so high we didn't even hear it, but it leveled trees all the way down the coast, even the top of my own white birch tree. Wilson was sure the village had been flattened and he called Eric at Powell River.

"What have you done with my sister?" he asked. "Have you made her a blood brother of the tribe?"

Eric laughed, he said I was at Kingcome and planning to leave the next day. I would stay several days with him in Powell River and then start home.

Ron and Dorothy took me to Alert Bay. I remember one girl whose husband drank too much, couldn't learn to budget and was pursued by bad luck, who begged us to take her along so she could borrow money from relatives at Alert Bay. She was not a princess, but she, too, was gentle and sweet and appealing. Of course we took her.

We tied up at Alert Bay and the next morning we had breakfast with Captain Nicholson and his lovely English wife. We saw his ship, of course.

The operating room was small but complete.

"Enough plaster of paris to fix all the broken legs in Canada," one of the crew told me. The crew had a fine system of choosing the cook. When a new crewman came aboard they served him an awful meal. If he complained, he was unanimously elected cook.

We saw the fine totems in the Indian cemetery at Alert Bay in the rain.

Ron took me by the only taxi to a tiny seaplane and said, "It will take only four and sometimes the door won't stay shut. You may have to sit on somebody's lap, but you will like it."

I thanked him and Dorothy for their goodness to me. Then I was on the little plane. We came to a place where a long cable was strung across the water. The plane ducked under it and stopped at a small, lonely float where three loggers got aboard. I sat on one's lap and all three entertained me royally.

"See that mountainside? Last year a plane like this one crashed against it and killed everybody aboard."

As I left Kingcome, I remembered that several Indians had told me about the movie star's yacht that had tied up in the inlet. The Americans had found a forestry boat to take them to the village and snooped everywhere, talking about their large church in Hollywood. When they were gone, one of the boys had drawn a dollar bill on the sand with his foot and he had said, "An American stood here." I had thanked them profusely and said I would use the story.

When I finally arrived at Powell River after a stop at Campbell River, there was Eric, all smiles.

"We are waiting dinner for you," he said. "The bishop and his wife are coming tomorrow."

The bishop was a remarkable man. His lovely wife had some Indian blood. At church the next morning she said to me, "The kneelers in this church at Powell River are very hard, don't you think so?"

"I have never been to church three times in one day," I said. "I don't dare look down. I think I have blistered both my knees. You know, I think I will put up a sign 'An American kneeled here.'" She laughed and so did I. Touché!

I stayed three days in Powell River. Eric and I discussed everything I had seen and he told me much of his first days in the village.

One night when the boys were at work in the pulp mill he asked me if I thought the book would sell. I said that the famous old *Post* editor who did the buying had told me that if you did a story well enough, it would go no matter what.

The last night I was there I took all the boys to dinner. In the morning when I left, after working all night in the pulp mill, there they were with Eric to see me off.

Not once during my visit had anyone said to me, "Oh, you mustn't say that." Or "You mustn't say this. It will offend someone." They had left me absolutely free to write about Kingcome as I saw it. They had not even asked what I was going to write.

When the plane left they were all smiling and waving. The tears were rolling down my cheeks.

I had been gone nearly four months. After Kingcome's cold, Sacramento's late fall felt warm.

"I thought you would wire," Wilson said, as he let me in.

"I knew if I did you would be up all night worrying."

We raided the icebox and talked and talked. I had come home from another world.

It took me a month to copy the random notes I had made. I spent another two months turning all the notes around in my mind trying to find the place to begin in such richness of material.

There was one part of the upper river I had not seen because of the weather, so Eric flew to Sacramento and drew a picture of it for me with every detail. We took him to the Mother Lode and showed him a bit of our own country, Wilson teasing us incessantly about our preoccupation with the book.

One day I made a timetable of the yearly pattern of the tribe. September, the spawning of the salmon. October, the shake cabins up the river where the fish were smoked. November, the hospital ship comes to the village and the vicarage becomes a clinic. And the small children hide. The doctor on the hospital ship had to pull teeth and he was seldom adept. Christmas, snow and carols, the young people going around the village singing. Trips with gifts for the isolated hand loggers. January, storms, clamming when the tide was out. The beginning of the famous dances holding the deepest and oldest beliefs of the tribe. February, very cold and windy. March, the coming of the oolachon—the candlefish—and the rendering of the *gleena* (Indian honey) with which the Indian flavors his food. April, birds, buds, seals and spring. May, jigging for halibut. July, gill-netting in the inlet. The children home from school, in and out of the water all day long.

I had a pattern. I fitted my notes into the yearly cycle. The ancient, the new, all the incidents I had seen and been told by everyone.

When Eric returned he wrote that the Canadian Navy had sent a destroyer to visit Kingcome. The destroyer was moored in the inlet and the crew taken by canoe to the village. It was a day of sports and keen competition and the Indians licked the navy to the finish at everything. Lieutenant Governor Pearkness was made a member of the tribe, hereafter known, in Indian of course, as "Chief Big Mountain." He made a speech I wish I had heard. "My people," he said to the Indians, and to the crew, "You palefaces"—the Indians loved it.

I knew one thing sure when I started work on my novel, *I Heard the Owl Call My Name*, and I didn't like it. I was going to kill off Mark Brian, the Anglican priest. I wasted twenty starts trying to avoid it. In my mind Eric was already a member of my blessed infantry. He bore his broken back with the same courage and grace, the same humor, but he was in no danger of death. I think my decision was based on something Eric told me the bishop had said to him when he asked him to go to Kingcome.

"The Indian knows his village as no white man knows his own land or even his own country. But there is one thing you must know. No matter how well you do, he will never thank you. There is no word for 'thank you' in Kwakwala."

Often in the avalanche of letters I received after the novel was published, people asked me what disease killed Mark Brian. I don't know. What matters is that he learned more of love and life in his three years with the Indians than most men learn in a long lifetime, and that it was he who thanked them.

I knew that when the book reached the village Eric and the boys would stay up all night to see which Indians I had used for characters. All the village was in the book, but I had changed their names. I had given Keetah her Indian name, but she was made up of several of the girls I had come to love. Eric wrote me that Ernest Willie, one of the boys working in the pulp mill to go to college, said slowly, "She has written a masterpiece of our people."

I did, however, put in two characters that could be recognized. When I sent him a copy, I wrote the bishop the book was for the tribe and for him, also. "I tried my best to make you a nice, plump, short, jolly bishop," I said, "but I couldn't do a thing with you."

There was one other exception. The anthropologist who called the tribe "Quackadoodles" was an Englishman. I turned him into a woman in a thick wool suit with a very tight skirt and huge flat shoes, who mispronounced everything. I knew they would recognize me and laugh. The only reason I didn't have me step into the ice water up to my armpits as the Englishman had done was because I knew it would take six hours to thaw me out, if ever, as I had learned.

I Heard the Owl Call My Name was turned down by every American publisher but bought in Canada, where it was an immediate best-seller. Demands for it came down over the border with Americans who had read it in Canada. The salesman for Doubleday urged his publisher to buy the American rights, which they did, years after the Canadian publication.

When the movie was made, the best Canadian director did it. The cast was excellent, but so much time had gone by that when they went to Kingcome to make the picture it was no more.

Two or three of the Indians who couldn't handle their liquor, who kept their checks in a coffee can and who hired a seaplane to come take them out when they needed more to drink were the only ones left. A fire had destroyed several houses. The beaches were filthy, covered with garbage. Indian boys called "flower children" by Canadians and "hippies" by us had destroyed the signs of the ancient potlatches on the granite side of the inlet. Since there was no place to house the cast or crew, the picture was made at a village on the western side of Vancouver Island. People who had not read the book liked it, but I, of course, did not recognize one bit of the village or the people I had come to love.

I Heard the Owl Call My Name sold over a million copies and was translated into ten or twelve languages.

I remember walking along the streets of London and passing a bookstore that featured the *Publisher's Monthly*, a magazine about the size of *Time*, in the entire window. The *Publisher's Monthly*'s cover was the "Owl," in brown and yellow.

"This little book," the cover read, "with a minimum of fuss, has become an international classic."

I didn't buy one. I was too awed. But in the

British Isles from the north of Scotland to Wales I bumped into the "Owl" constantly. Even in the small villages where there were no libraries and a motortruck came weekly with books, there was the "Owl," usually sitting on top of the stack.

There was an astounding deluge of mail. There were hundreds and hundreds of letters from all over the world. From the rich and the poor, the House of Commons, boys in jail, Arabs, Africans, a headhunter village in New Guinea, from Australia, New Zealand and of course from Canada and my own country.

It is strange when a professional creative writer turns out a story that becomes so successful. It is not the critics who let him know. It is the readers.

The vast majority of the readers of *I Heard the Owl Call My Name* said the same thing in almost the same words: "I have read the 'Owl' four times and I feel I must write and tell you what it means to me."

No form letter was adequate. I wrote small personal notes and thanked each of them.

For years Kingcome was all but deserted. The tribe had crossed the bridge into the white man's world of modern wonders and marvelous gadgets.

When Kingcome was deserted, Eric's work in Canada changed greatly. The Indians settled at Alert Bay, at Campbell River and in Vancouver. They met, and kept up their old crafts. Eric continued to see them, of course. He was asked to be the bishop of the Yukon, but his own bishop refused to let him go because of his back. Now he did considerable work with white boys, also. If a white boy got himself into serious trouble, Eric was the one he trusted. There was no filth, degradation he didn't hear, and there was no one else they trusted as they trusted him.

One day I had from Eric an astounding phone call. Slowly, the Indians were beginning to drift back to Kingcome.

"They have begun to realize that however well they do in the white man's world, nothing can replace their own deep roots that reach back so many hundreds of years. The culture has changed greatly, but it holds the deepest meaning of their lives. Loneliness has always been an element they know and they have lived in it superbly. The white man's culture can never take its place, nor can they ever become completely part of his culture. Seventy Indians have returned to the village of Quee, 'the inside place.'"

"Do they render *gleena*—they used to call it Indian honey—and use it to flavor their food, and when rendering it—"

"You can smell it for miles and miles and it's as awful as ever.

"Margaret, the last time I was there one of the Indians wished to talk to me of the tragic death of a relative and his two sons. He said, 'I saw two young wolves across the river the day before the bad news came and I knew that Dan and his sons had gone to the land of the wolves.'"

"Are the beaches clean again?" I asked.

"Yes, and the young men chop wood on the beaches and check their nets to see what they have caught. At night the gaslights burn and the coffee smells warm and the men tell the old stories and play the old games."

"How is Ron?"

"Ron and Dorothy have two lovely children and have done well.

"And guess what? Ernest Willie, who represented the Indian people in Toronto, has returned now to help in the reorganization of his own tribe. The Anglican church has adopted a new attitude toward alcohol, the 'courage in a bottle' too many Indians use to face the white man's world. We are treating it now as a medical problem, as long ago we treated smallpox, syphilis and TB. Canada has closed its border to immigration. It welcomes tourists but not those who would stay."

"It's a miracle," I said.

"It is indeed. You haven't heard it all," Eric said. "Listen to this. On Queen Victoria Day, which the Indians celebrate because she said 'Wherever you see clam shells, it means Indian country—leave it alone,' after thirty years they gave me a new name. I am now called 'Large Copper.'

"Three hundred Indians gathered at King-come to hold a memorial for three Indians lost at sea.

"We have had many visitors, the Archbishop from Scotland, a Bishop from Kent, even the Archbishop of Canterbury, and government officials sending men on some difficult tasks. Every important visitor who comes will say: 'Do you know Margaret Craven?' and I'll laugh and say, 'I do indeed.'

"Margaret, in some strange way you have become part of this country. The people always ask for you. 'How is Margaret now?' 'What is she doing?' 'Is she coming back to us?'"

This, I think, has given me greater pleasure than any other I have received from the book.

*　　*　　*

I had one more book I wanted to write, of the lovely summers in the Cascades of my childhood, of my father's days in Montana when it was the last great adventure, of the closeness, the safety, the old integrity that now is almost gone.

Walk Gently This Good Earth is as true as *I Heard the Owl Call My Name*, but it is true with a difference, and of a different generation. A professional writer must be careful what he writes now about the past which could be used to hurt innocent people unmercifully.

I like young people. I think it is time my country does what the Indians of Kingcome are doing. We must return to our own roots, our own safety and integrity, and I think this is beginning to occur. Our lives depend upon it.

Richard Hooker wrote well of the reason people spend their lives learning to write:

Though for no other cause, yet for this,
That posterity may know we have
Not loosely through silence
Permitted things to pass away as in a dream.